first book of

baby
animals

Isabel Thomas

A & C BLACK
AN IMPRINT OF BLOOMSBURY
LONDON NEW DELHI NEW YORK SYDNEY

Published 2014 by
A&C Black
An imprint of Bloomsbury Publishing Plc
50 Bedford Square, London, WC1B 3DP

www.bloomsbury.com

ISBN 978-1-4729-0400-3

This book is produced using paper that is made from wood
grown in managed, sustainable forests. It is natural, renewable
and recyclable. The logging and manufacturing processes
conform to the environmental regulations of the country of origin.

Printed in China by Leo Paper Products, Heshan, Guangdong

10 9 8 7 6 5 4 3 2 1

Contents

Baby animals

Baby animals are all around us. Look out for cute, cuddly, clumsy baby animals in all sorts of shapes and sizes.

You can spot baby animals in parks, gardens, and in the countryside. You can see others at farms, wildlife parks, and zoos. This book will help you to learn about the different baby animals you see. It tells you some special features to look out for.

At the back of this book is a Spotter's Guide to help you remember the baby animals you spot. Tick them off as you see them. You can also find out the meaning of some useful words.

Turn the page to find out all about baby animals!

Barn owl

Most baby barn owls hatch in spring. Their mother keeps them warm until they are covered in soft down. Owlets like to play. They run, jump, and twist their heads.

Hungry owlets call loudly as they wait for their parents to bring food.

Fluffy white down

Heart-shaped face

A baby bird's soft fluffy feathers are called down.

Blue whale

Blue whale calves are the world's biggest babies. A newborn calf can weigh more than

Blue whales are mammals, so calves drink their mother's milk.

two cars. They grow two-and-a-half centimetres longer every day.

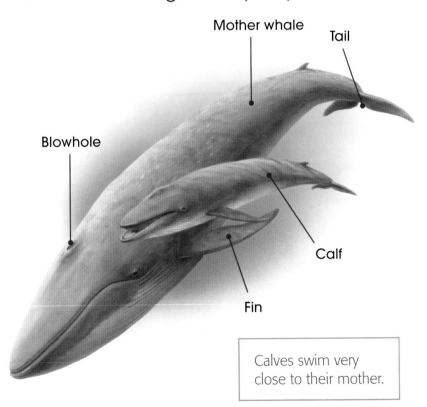

Mother whale

Tail

Blowhole

Calf

Fin

Calves swim very close to their mother.

Brown bear

Brown bear cubs are born in winter, in underground dens. They stay inside their den with their mother until spring.

Round ears

Brown bear cubs like to climb trees.

Long claws

Shaggy brown fur

The mother bear protects her cubs. She chases away dangerous animals.

Butterfly

Look closely at leaves to spot tiny butterfly eggs.

Caterpillars eat the leaf they were born on first.

These eggs hatch into caterpillars. The caterpillars eat and eat. They grow quickly.

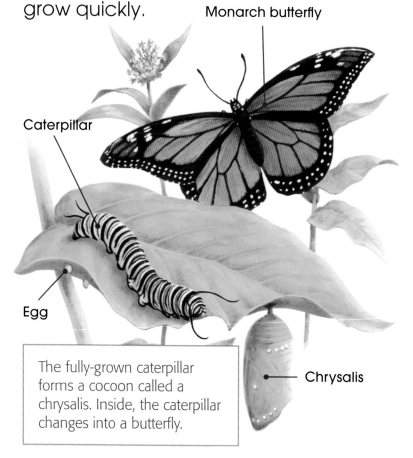

Monarch butterfly

Caterpillar

Egg

The fully-grown caterpillar forms a cocoon called a chrysalis. Inside, the caterpillar changes into a butterfly.

Chrysalis

Camel

Baby camels are born without humps. At first they only drink their mother's milk. Their fatty humps grow when they start eating plants.

Baby camels often have white fur. Most turn brown as they get older, but some camels stay white.

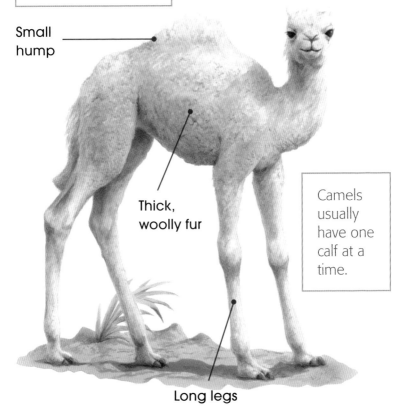

Small hump

Thick, woolly fur

Camels usually have one calf at a time.

Long legs

Cat

Baby cats are called kittens. They love to play and explore. Their mother carries them back if they stray too far.

Kittens like to scratch and nip things. This is how they learn about the world.

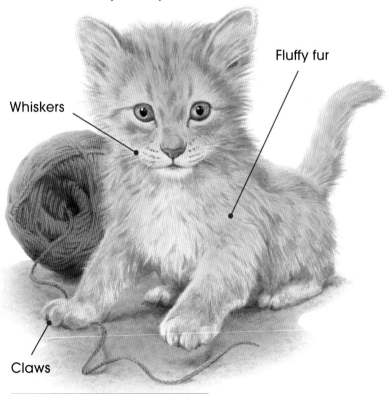

Fluffy fur

Whiskers

Claws

The mother cat licks her kittens to clean their fur.

Chicken

Chicks grow inside eggs. After three weeks, they peck their way out. The mother hen keeps her chicks warm until their feathers are dry and fluffy.

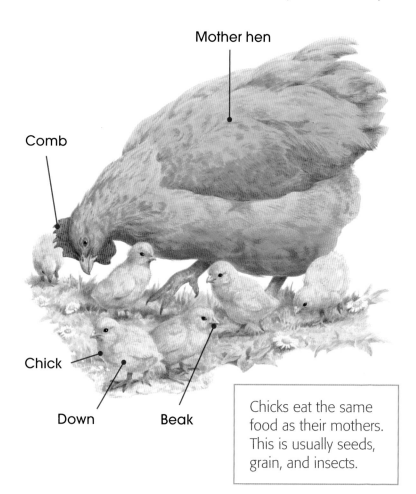

Mother hen

Comb

Chick

Down

Beak

Chicks eat the same food as their mothers. This is usually seeds, grain, and insects.

Chimpanzee

A baby chimp's favourite games are tickling, chasing, and wrestling. Baby chimps laugh, smile, and giggle as they play.

Spot baby chimps by looking for a tuft of white hair on their bottoms.

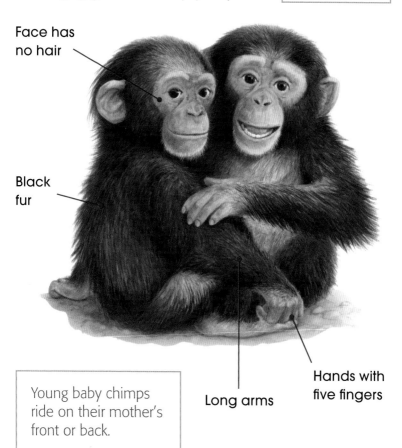

Face has no hair

Black fur

Long arms

Hands with five fingers

Young baby chimps ride on their mother's front or back.

13

Cow

Most calves are born in springtime. At first they stay very close to their mothers. Older calves love to play. They jump, kick, and gallop around fields in groups.

Mother cows take it in turns to watch the calves as they play.

Crocodile

Baby crocodiles grow inside eggs. When they hatch, they climb straight into their

Baby crocodiles make loud chirping and squeaking sounds.

mother's huge jaws! She gently carries them to the water. Baby crocodiles can swim as soon as they hatch.

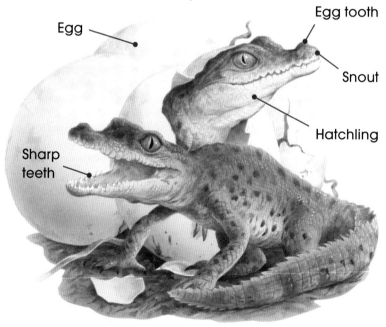

Egg

Egg tooth

Snout

Hatchling

Sharp teeth

Baby crocodiles have a hard patch at the tip of their snout. They use it to break out of their egg.

Deer

Baby deer are called fawns. You might spot a fawn in spring, if you walk quietly through a forest or wood. Look carefully because fawns are very good at hiding.

This fawn's spotted coat helps it to blend in with the forest.

Large ears

Black nose and eyes

Spotted coat

Dog

Newborn puppies cannot see or hear. They spend most of their time

It takes a year for a puppy to become a grown-up dog.

sleeping. Puppies grow up fast. After four weeks they start playing and learning about the world.

Golden retriever puppy

Large paws

Tail

Just like you, puppies get milk teeth before they get their grown-up teeth.

Duck

Look out for ducklings in spring and early summer. They bob around in the water looking for small animals and plants to eat. Listen out for mother ducks quacking loudly to call their ducklings back.

As soon as the ducklings hatch, the mother duck leads them into the water.

Mallard duck

Soft down

Ducks usually lay nine eggs at once.

Duckling

Elephant

Baby elephants have a wobbly, floppy trunk at first. They can't pick anything up. The calves learn how to use their trunk as they grow. This takes lots of practise.

Baby elephants have milk tusks. They get wobbly and fall out, just like milk teeth.

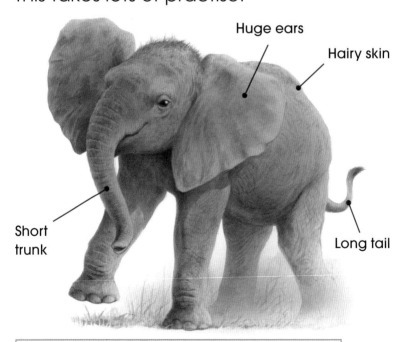

Huge ears

Hairy skin

Short trunk

Long tail

Elephants live in herds. The whole herd helps to look after baby elephants and keep them safe.

Emperor penguin

Emperor penguins live in the coldest part of the world. Young chicks keep warm by standing on a parent's feet, and snuggling against their tummy.

Emperor penguins lay one egg at a time.

Chick

Emperor penguins do not build nests. The father penguin balances the egg on his feet. He keeps the egg warm until it hatches.

Fluffy grey down

Flamingo

Flamingo chicks don't look like their parents when they hatch. They have white or grey feathers and a straight bill.

Flamingo chicks gather in huge groups to stay safe. Parents come back to feed their chicks. They tell which chick is theirs by listening out for its call.

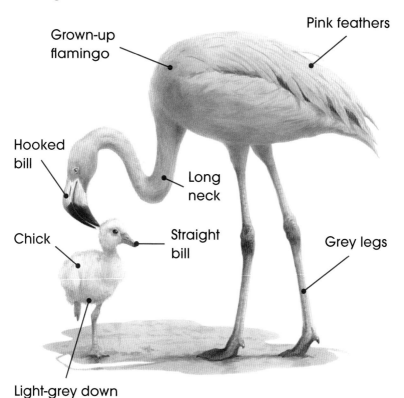

Grown-up flamingo

Pink feathers

Hooked bill

Long neck

Chick

Straight bill

Grey legs

Light-grey down

 # Fox

Fox cubs are born in spring. The mother fox keeps her cubs warm. After a few weeks, the cubs start to play. Fox cubs love chasing each other, playing tug-of-war, and pretending to fight.

Large, pointed ears

Black nose

Black fur

The other foxes in the family all help to bring food for the cubs.

Frog

Look out for ponds full of frogspawn in spring. The frogspawn hatches into tadpoles. The tadpoles change into froglets. The tiny froglets crawl out of the water onto land.

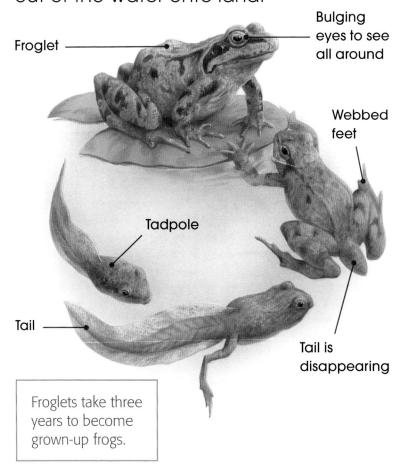

Froglet

Bulging eyes to see all around

Webbed feet

Tadpole

Tail

Tail is disappearing

Froglets take three years to become grown-up frogs.

Giant panda

Panda cubs are very clumsy. They learn how to roll when they fall over, for a soft landing. Mother pandas love playing with their cubs.

Panda cubs are born with white fur. Their black patches start to grow when they are a week old.

Black eyes and ears

Black and white markings

White face

Cubs learn to eat bamboo by copying their mother.

Giraffe

Newborn giraffes are the world's tallest babies. They are about the same height as a door. At first calves hide near their mother. She protects them from animals such as lions and leopards.

Giraffe calves make bleating and mewing sounds.

Horns covered in skin

Large ears

Long neck

Spotted coat

Older calves spend the day in groups. The mother giraffes take it in turns to watch over the babies.

Long legs

 # Goat

Baby goats are called kids. They love to have fun climbing. Head-butting is another baby goat game. Watch out for those growing horns!

Most baby goats have a twin brother or sister.

Growing horns

Small tail

Hoof

Kids chew everything they can. This is how they find out about the world.

Harp seal

Harp seal pups are born on the Arctic ice. Their woolly white fur keeps them warm. The pups stay on the ice while they grow silvery-grey fur.

Mother harp seals leave their babies on the ice while they catch fish. They come back to feed their babies milk.

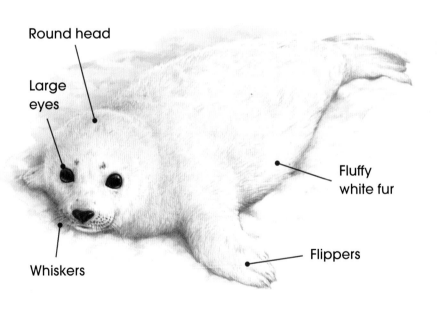

Round head

Large eyes

Whiskers

Fluffy white fur

Flippers

Once the pups grow silvery-grey fur, they can dive into the water to look for their own food.

Hippo

Hippos are often born in water.
The mother hippo and her calf stay
in the water until the calf is strong
enough to walk and run on land.

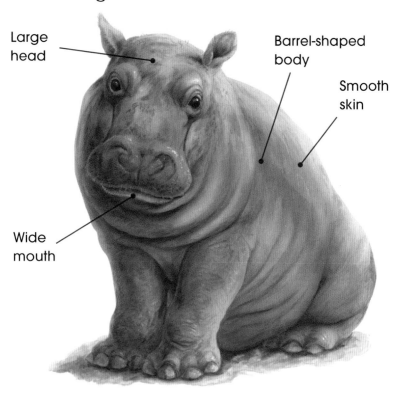

Large
head

Barrel-shaped
body

Smooth
skin

Wide
mouth

Mother hippos love cuddling
up to their babies. They even
babysit for other hippos.

Horse

Baby horses are called foals. They have very strong legs. They can stand up an hour after they are born, walk after two hours, and trot and gallop after four hours.

Foals have very long legs for their size. They have to bend their knees to nibble grass.

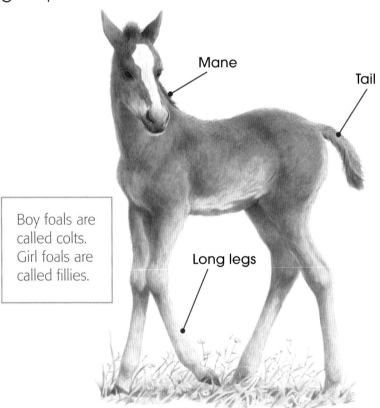

Mane

Tail

Boy foals are called colts. Girl foals are called fillies.

Long legs

Kangaroo

Baby kangaroos are called joeys. They love playing wrestling, boxing, and hopping games. If they spot danger, they jump into their mother's pouch.

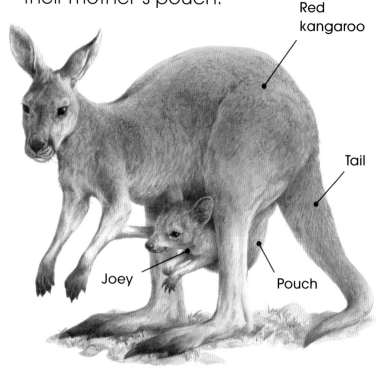

Red kangaroo

Tail

Joey

Pouch

Newborn baby kangaroos are smaller than your little finger. They crawl into their mother's pouch and stay there until they are much bigger.

Koala

When a baby koala is born it weighs about as much as a raisin. The tiny joey crawls into its mother's pouch. It

After seven months, joeys are big enough to live outside the pouch. They ride around on their mother's back.

stays there for more than half a year.

Furry ears

Big black nose

Grey fur

You can only spot wild koalas in Australia.

Hands with three fingers and two thumbs

Lion

Lion cubs start learning how to hunt when they are six weeks old. They follow their mother wherever she goes. They copy what she does.

Male lions have huge shaggy manes. These start to grow when the boy cubs are one year old.

Yellow-brown coat

Lion cubs are born with spotty fur.

Spots

Mouse

A mother mouse has up to 120 babies every year! They are born with no hair apart from their whiskers. The tiny babies are called pinkies. Their furry coats grow after ten days.

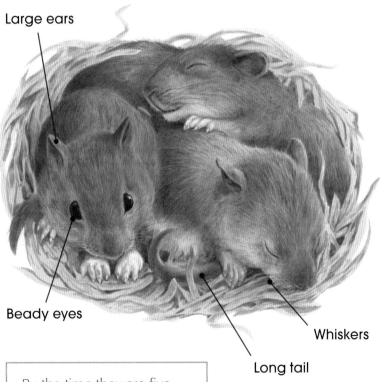

Large ears

Beady eyes

Long tail

Whiskers

By the time they are five weeks old, mice are ready to have babies of their own!

Pig

Piglets drink their mother's milk. They feed once every hour. This helps them to grow quickly. In just one week their weight doubles!

A curly tail can be a sign that a piglet is happy.

Ear

Snout

Curly tail

Trotter

Up to ten brothers and sisters can be born at the same time.

Rabbit

Baby rabbits are called kittens. When they are born they can't see or hear. Their eyes open after two weeks. Then they start to explore the world outside their nest.

Look out for baby rabbits springing into the air as they play.

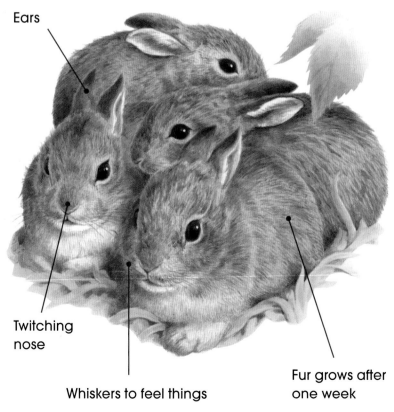

Ears

Twitching nose

Whiskers to feel things

Fur grows after one week

Raccoon

Imagine being born in a tree, sewer, or attic! Mother raccoons build dens in any safe place they can find. They make a soft nest for their kits.

Kits make a whining sound like puppies.

Black furry 'mask'

Five long toes

The kits live with their mother for more than a year. They do everything together.

Tail rings

Seahorse

Father seahorses have a special pouch. The mother seahorse lays her eggs in the pouch. The father seahorse looks after the eggs until they hatch.

More than 1000 babies can be born at once.

Fins for steering

Snout

Fin for swimming

The baby seahorses are called fry.

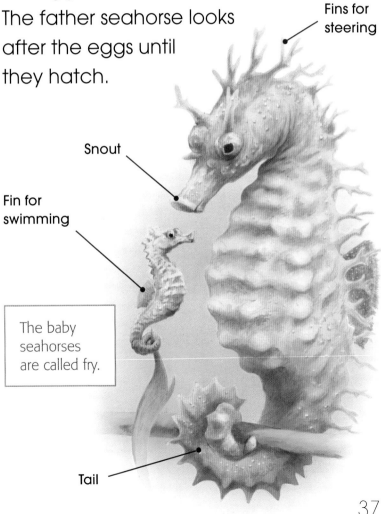

Tail

 # Shark

Some baby sharks hatch out of eggs. Others grow inside their mother's tummy. The babies are called pups. They look just like grown-up sharks, but they are much smaller.

This is a newborn lemon shark pup. It lives in shallow water at first, to keep away from larger sharks.

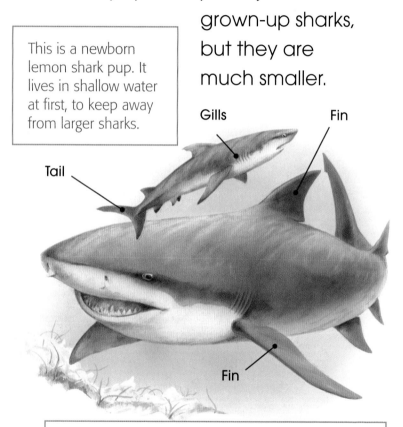

Gills

Fin

Tail

Fin

A shark's egg is known as a mermaid's purse. It is tough, to protect the baby shark growing inside.

Sheep

Lambs are born in the springtime. They can stand up after just a few minutes. Lambs drink milk from their mother until they are old enough to eat grass.

Listen out for lambs bleating loudly. This is how they call for help.

Mother sheep (ewe)

Woolly coat

Hoof

Lambs love to play together.

Two-month old lamb

 # Swan

Baby swans are called cygnets. The mother and father swan look after their cygnets together. Look out for swans carrying cygnets on their backs, or under their wings.

Fluffy grey-brown down

Dark-grey beak

Mute swan

Swan families often swim in a line, with one parent at the front and one at the back.

Animal groups

Amphibians

Baby amphibians hatch from eggs. They live in water. As they grow, their bodies change so they can breathe air and live on land.

Birds

Birds have feathers, wings, and a beak. Baby birds hatch from eggs with hard shells. Their parents look after them very well.

Fish

Fish have fins for swimming, and gills to breathe underwater. Baby fish usually hatch from eggs laid in the water.

Insects

Insects are small animals with six legs. They often have wings. Most baby insects hatch from eggs.

Mammals

Mammals have hair or fur. Most baby mammals grow inside their mother's tummy. When they are born, their mother makes milk to feed them.

Reptiles

Reptiles have dry, scaly skin. At first, they lay eggs with soft shells. Baby reptiles hatch from the eggs. They can already look after themselves.

Spotter's guide

How many of these baby animals
have you seen? Tick them when
you spot them.

☐ Barn owl
page 6

☐ Blue whale
page 7

☐ Brown bear
page 8

☐ Butterfly
page 9

☐ Camel
page 10

☐ Cat
page 11

Chicken
page 12

Chimpanzee
page 13

Cow
page 14

Crocodile
page 15

Deer
page 16

Dog
page 17

Duck
page 18

Elephant
page 19

☐ **Hippo**
page 28

☐ **Horse**
page 29

☐ **Kangaroo**
page 30

☐ **Koala**
page 31

☐ **Lion**
page 32

☐ **Mouse**
page 33

☐ **Pig**
page 34

☐ **Rabbit**
page 35

Useful words

hatch to come out of an egg

herd a large group of animals that live together

pouch a pocket in a mother kangaroo or koala's tummy, for carrying very young babies

Find out more

If you would like to find out more about baby animals, start with these websites and books. You can look at pictures and videos of baby animals, and find out where to spot baby animals near you.

National Geographic Kids
www.nationalgeographic.co.uk/kids

BBC Nature
www.bbc.co.uk/nature

Zoological Society of London Kids
www.zsl.org/kids

My First Book of Baby Animals
by Mike Unwin (Bloomsbury, 2014)